REMARRIAGE AFTER 50

REMARRIAGE AFTER 50

WHAT WOMEN, MEN
AND ADULT CHILDREN
NEED TO KNOW

BY

JANE HUGHES BARTON

Library of Congress Cataloguing-in-Publication Data

Barton, Jane Hughes.
  Remarriage After 50: what women, men and adult children need to know / by Jane Hughes Barton

  p. cm.

  ISBN 0-9639891-0-3

    1. Remarriage. 2. Marriage. 3. Middle-aged persons.
    I. Title.
    HQ1018.B37 1994   306.8'4
                            QB193-22590

Published by Roger-Thomas Press
Box 1563
Fort Walton Beach, FL 32548

Printed in the United States of America
Book design and production by Kramer Communications
Printed on recycled paper by Thomson-Shore
Second printing, 1994

To my second husband
and
To my sons and their families
for their love and support of both of us

CONTENTS

ACKNOWLEDGMENTS

To the many people who have encouraged me during the years I have been writing this book, and have given of their expertise, I give my heartfelt thanks.

Stanley S. Heller, M.D.; David E. Mulford, D.Min; Shirley Longshore and Muriel Jorgensen, editors; Judith Appelbaum and Sensible Solutions; Francis X. O'Brien, Esq.; Robert R. Thompson, Esq.; Bert Schwartz, Ph.D.; Carole and C.J. Everett; Shirley Horner; Rev. Thomas Tewell; Barbara Liston Leone; Donald Fowles; Barbara F. Wilson; Roldah Cameron; Betsy Potter; Susan Morris; Rev. Janice Smith Ammon; Barbara Morcheles; Norma Miller; Metropolitan Writers Group; International Women's Writing Guild.

And all the remarried women who shared their lives with me, whose names will never be revealed. This book could not have been written if they had not been willing to talk so openly with me.

Introduction

THE CASE FOR TAKING YOUR TIME

A COUNSELOR SPEAKS TO
THE READERS OF THIS BOOK

BY DAVID E. MULFORD, D.MIN.

A S A MINISTER serving a large church in Florida, where there are many older people, I am often asked to perform second and even third marriages. I talk with the couples before marriage and sometimes counsel them later on, and I am aware of what's going on in their relationship, whether it be good or not so good.

My conclusions come not from in-depth studies or statistical studies. What I say comes from particular situations I have dealt with and people I have known and counseled during my 37 years in the ministry.

Often, I observe the following: A man is widowed; perhaps he had been married for 40 years or more to the same person. He and his wife had a good relationship. They could work things out, and he felt content in his marriage. Now suddenly, or perhaps not so suddenly, he is all alone and he feels lost. In a number of instances, the man is eager to remarry quickly. He is lonely. It may be that what he is really looking for is someone to take care of him.

I remember talking with a friend whose wife had died. Soon afterward, he married a fine woman who had been his secretary. I always remember what he said to me: "I cannot really be alone. I just cannot deal with it emotionally." And that turned out to be a wonderful marriage. It went on for years, and she was of great assistance to him, and then she died and he was left alone again.

I have known people who went into marriage too quickly. The woman is quite delighted having someone in her life after having been alone, someone to take her out to shows, out to dinner — with all the wining and dining — she is very much taken up by that. She seems to be looking ahead and thinking, "Oh, isn't it nice this is going to continue."

After the marriage takes place, the couple finds out neither one knows the other well enough. The husband is expecting someone to take care of him, and the new wife isn't really interested in doing that at all. The wife is looking for someone to take her out and entertain her. All he really wants is to sit home and watch the ball game. There is a letdown, a disappointment. They realize they went into the marriage without knowing each other well.

I can think of some specific cases where the remarriage took place before the grieving process for the first spouse was over. When the loss of a spouse has not been worked through, a person isn't able to enter into a good, healthy relationship. The grieving process takes time.

There are various steps of grieving that one goes through in a loss. There is a feeling of being abandoned, even anger sometimes. I saw anger in a man whose first wife died. They had had a very happy relationship. He remarried too soon, and the second marriage was not at all good. Years later, he made the comment, "I don't know why she died." He was still angry, feeling that his first wife had deserted him.

The grieving process is necessary for good emotional health. It is hard to short-circuit mourning successfully. I can't tell you the number of months or years it takes, but working through the grief is essential. It means dealing with your feelings and letting some time go by. Then you will be ready to enter into a new relationship. This is equally important for men *and* women. Sometimes, people feel that another marriage will short-circuit the suffering. "If I marry again, then I'm going to be happy and I don't have to work through the grieving process." It's a mistake people make. It just doesn't work that way, however. They don't realize that grief is not something that can be tied up neatly in a short period of time.

People handle the grieving process in different ways. Some people work through it better than others. But when you see that somebody is still unable to even talk about a family member after years have gone by, chances are they have not worked through their grief successfully. Sometimes they never work through it; they are constantly mourning the loss of that person. There is a problem if one is not able to deal with the loss after a period of time. If one cannot get on with life, counseling may be beneficial.

"Working through it" simply means facing the reality of each day. You deal with it on a day-to-day, week-by-week, month-by-month basis. You take care of those things that must be taken care of. You are able to gradually emerge from your intense grieving and are able to socialize and to once again pick up responsibilities through the community and the church. You work through the process of getting over that feeling of loss, of missing that other individual, until you get back to what one would call a normal life pattern. Part of the process of working through it is letting some time go by and then getting back to where you can gradually pick up some of your previous activities. Life will take on some kind of normal pace again.

You know you are working through the loss when you can deal with life and feel that you can handle things fairly well. It is important not to make any important decisions, such as selling your house, right away. Sometimes people think, "Oh, I can't live in this place anymore." Then in a couple of months or so, you've sold your house. What you are saying is, "If I get out of these surroundings, I won't think about that other person. It will be easier." That is not dealing with the loss. Maybe the best thing to do is take a trip and enjoy that. If you make those big decisions early, you are trying to escape.

Instead, say, "This is the reality of this situation. I'm going to have to deal with it. I am going to muster up my old resources and the faith that I bring to it, my own philosophy of life and what gives me strength, and proceed. I will take care of things that need to be taken care of until I begin to feel somewhat at peace with myself and am able to put my mind on things that need to be done and are good to do, and do them well." On the other hand, thinking, "Well, if I get involved with another woman (or the woman gets involved with another man), it's going to help me" is another kind of escape.

You have to differentiate between what is an escape and what is a healthy way to work through the process. One of the things people do too quickly is remarry. There are lots of dangers involved.

When two people do make a decision to remarry, it is very important to work out financial arrangements in advance. If money is a taboo subject, you are not ready. It is important for a couple entering a second marriage to work out an arrangement for how they are going to handle the costs of living, a home, medical expenses, clothes, travel and other financial matters.

Money is the number one problem in first marriages. It

causes the most unrest and arguing. In second marriages, it is much more complicated. I always say to couples that it isn't so much the amount of money; it's the attitude toward money. To one partner, it may be how much you save that is important. To the other, it may be how much you spend. You need to have a meeting of the minds before you remarry.

What are some of the things that pave the way for a better relationship in a second marriage? There is the story of the minister who said, in preaching, "Now, if anyone in this congregation is perfect, I want that person to stand up." A man in the back of the church stood up. The minister said, "Why, I can't believe it! You mean you're perfect?" The man said, "No, it's not that. I'm standing up for my wife's first husband." That first husband was considered to have been absolutely perfect, and therefore, the second husband didn't have a chance.

This is a common occurrence. If you had a very happy marriage for 40 or 50 years and you have lost that spouse, the good memories tend to become stronger as time goes on, and the problems tend to fade in the distance. There is always the danger of idolizing the deceased spouse. When a person had a wonderfully happy marriage, and the first partner died, the danger is that the person expects the second partner to be a carbon copy of the first. One has to be careful about this. You don't have to close that chapter as if it never existed, but you do have to be sure not to lose sight of reality.

I knew a couple very well; the wife died when she was in her late forties, and I conducted the funeral. The husband, after a reasonable amount of time, married a lovely woman, and I participated in that wedding. When they married, they moved to another part of the country. He had an opportunity to go into business there. However, I think it was not just coincidental. His first wife was well-known; she was a social leader. He was a quieter person, but I think he felt if he stayed in the same community with the second wife, comparisons would be made to his first wife. So they moved. Much to my sadness, I learned that the second wife died a few years later.

I visited him a couple of times in his new home. He still is only in his mid-sixties, a widower twice. He has a beautiful home, lives alone, and doesn't know what he wants to do. One evening when I was visiting him, we took the dog out for a long walk and he said, "You know, if I remarried again, I would sell this house. I might not move a long way away, but I would move somewhere else." He wasn't really escaping. He felt it was better to start a new marriage in neutral territory than to stay in that house where he had memories of his previous wife. He said, "I have had two wonderful wives." He wonders, I think, if he can be that fortunate a third time.

Vera and David Mace, a wonderful couple, wrote a book, *To a Retired Couple* (Judson Press, 1985). They talk about those qualities that foster a happy retirement and also talk about second and third marriages. Two characteristics of the happily retired couple are creativity and service, referring to people who maintain a degree of creativity and people who see life as "not just what's in it for me, but how can I make a contribution." I think that says a lot about people who are married a second or third time. For those whose whole life is centered on themselves and their own entertainment, something is missing. That affects a marriage relationship.

I think of a second marriage that was entered into too quickly and didn't work out. It was a disaster. I knew the husband, and as his daughter said, "He really had no interest outside himself." The man was a goodhearted fellow, but all his interests were centered on himself, and he had no resources to turn to. I think he went into the remarriage thinking it would meet all his needs and solve all his problems.

If you are a creative person and a service-oriented person, you bring a level of vitality, interest and outward direction to a second or third marriage that is healthy. You have things in the right perspective and are a better candidate for remarriage than someone who does nothing but watch television and count out his money. A good candidate has a healthy outlook on life, a good balance.

We need to nurture our own inner being, our own spiritual life. If you don't have that, you don't have inner roots. But you also need to be outward-directed, or you are missing an important part of life. I believe people who nurture themselves in a healthy way and also reach out and are concerned about church, community and neighbors, have a healthy balance in life and are by far the better partners.

The issues of working through grief and developing outside interests apply to both men and women. But I do think men have a tendency to remarry sooner because they need someone to take care of them as well as needing companionship. And women know how to maintain the home. Also, a single man may feel that if he wants to marry again, it is easy for him to do so simply because of the numbers involved. There are more women than men who are single as we get older.

For divorced people, it helps if they have an understanding of why the first marriage didn't work out, so that history doesn't repeat itself. They need to understand the extent to which they are responsible. If they have self-learning or counseling experience, then I think they can make fine candidates for a remarriage.

Second or third marriages can be good, even great, and they can be a big blessing for lots of people. If you face the problems, and look for ways of solving them, you have a better chance of a happy relationship. I sincerely believe this book will help in making this important decision.

1

WHO WILL DARN MY SOCKS?

THE VULNERABILITY OF LIVING ALONE

A MAN WHO was an old friend called me a few months after his wife died. He said he thought he would marry again. He was 80. I asked why. He said, "Who will darn my socks?" I said, "No one will darn socks." And he asked what he was to do with them. I said, "Throw them in the wastebasket and go to the men's store and buy eight pairs of socks, all the same style and color." That solved his marriage problem, and some lucky woman's, too!

Another man I'd just met and talked to for five minutes said, "My wife divorced me after forty-five years of marriage.

I've got to get married or I'll starve to death." Love is not in the picture. These men want someone to take care of them.

One million people over 50 years old remarry every four years in the United States, according to the National Center for Health Statistics' latest survey. But since 1980, the number of divorced people over 65 has increased at an astounding rate. The American Association of Retired Persons' 1993 report, "A Profile of Older Americans," stated that, although divorced older persons over 64 represented only 5% of all older persons in 1992, their numbers (1.6 million divorced) had increased three times as fast as this older population as a whole since 1980.

In 1992, half of all women over 64 were widows. There were five times as many widows as widowers, according to a study by Donald Fowles for the U.S. Administration on Aging done in 1993. Perhaps it was put more bluntly in the same agency's 1991 report called "Aging America": "Women die widowed. Men die married."

We are vulnerable when we are first living alone. The death of a long-time partner, or a divorce (especially if it is unwanted), leaves a deep emotional wound. Loneliness can be overwhelming at times. Healing takes time, and mourning is a necessary part of the process. It may take a widow who had a good marriage five years or more to heal emotionally. Men, in general, recover more quickly. Many men are married again within two years. I think this is one of the reasons the adult children of widowed men often don't accept the second wife — the children have not completed their mourning.

I became a widow at 60 and married a widower two years later. Although I am an intelligent college graduate, I was not aware that remarriage at this stage of life is very *complicated*. And there was no book to guide me; such books are written for young couples with children and stepchildren at home. My second husband and I have built a good marriage of many years.

Now I have made a study of the subject and written this book. It is not a ponderous sociological study, but rather a short, easy-to-read summary of potential trouble spots in re-marriage after 50, as shown in interviews with women who have been through the experience. The book provides practical advice on how to deal with these "danger zones."

I interviewed 30 women who remarried after age 50 in eight states across the country to discover how they handled the challenges of a new, older-age marriage. They were contacted through senior citizens' centers, secretaries of clergy and friends of friends. Those who responded are of middle- and upper-middle-class backgrounds, about half of them college graduates, all fine, intelligent women.

I found that older men and women remarry for different reasons. Men want someone to take care of them, make a new home and cook for them. Women want a man to date — to be taken out for dinner — and for affection. And women want lovemaking.

Stories of 15 of the women are woven throughout the book, illustrating the subject of the chapter. Five of them remarried in their fifties, five in their sixties, and five in their seventies.

All had been remarried at least three years when interviewed, most between nine and 18 years, except two who divorced within 18 months. None had children living at home.

The quality of the marriages varies tremendously. Some are very good, some very bad, and a few are in between. One of the women experienced violence in her second marriage to a very "nice" man. Another found her husband had a longstanding problem with alcohol. Why have some women made the wrong choices?

"The most important quality in any marriage is the emotional health of each person," said Stanley S. Heller, M.D., a distinguished psychiatrist, who was selected as one of the top psychiatrists in New York City, according to a report in *New York* magazine. In three of the successful marriages, the women had previously been widowed or divorced for 15 to 20 years and were independent. Women in marriages that were difficult said they expected this one would be the same as their first marriage. But, another marriage will always be different.

There are four main differences in remarriage after 50: aging (including sexual and health changes), retirement with a new person, new adult children who may be interested in an estate, and people who are set in their ways of living.

There is an unwritten rule that a widowed or divorced person should not make a major change, such as selling a house, for at least a year, to be sure of using good judgment. When moving, there is a loss of self-image and familiar surroundings, particularly for a woman who has created the home. It is comforting to be in the same place with warm memories. And moving is lots of work. You don't need any more stress.

A woman reading this book should not feel comfortable. It is written so she, as well as men and adult children, will be aware of problems that may lie ahead and be prepared to deal with them.

A basic problem for a mature single woman is that there are very few single men from whom to choose, and it is often difficult to know much about the person's background. We do not know the parents of the intended because they are no longer living. Nor do we know his siblings intimately, if at all.

Many of the women interviewed were casual about their own financial arrangements in preparation for their remarriage. They let the men take over.

I only interviewed women for this book because I wanted to find out what women's lives are like in a new marriage to an older, possibly retired, man. Remarriage is harder for older women than men, the women said. Women and men have different expectations in later remarriage.

For one thing, a man, who often remarries within two years, wants a wife to prepare meals, make a new home, plan the social life, and be hospitable to his family and friends, in addition to her own financial responsibilities, activities and her family. A man may want a second wife who also contributes financially with her home, clothes, and her medical care.

Furthermore, men may face such problems as impotency and retirement, which affect their wives also and add stress to the marriage. Many women who remarried after 60 said they are working harder than when raising preschool children at home. These women are no longer young. Unlike men, the women now have new responsibilities for two families instead of one — twice as many people.

My friend **Pat** reiterated this in our interview. I knew Pat in college, where she was president of our class. Now, many years later, I saw her in her attractive condo in a suburb of San Francisco. She was 54 when she married the second time. Now she has been widowed twice. Pat is a secure woman who knows what she's doing; she's in charge of herself. It was wonderful to be with her again.

"A couple of my friends are widows and live in Sun City, Arizona, and they have dates," she told me. "They say, 'These men want to marry us. No way, José, I say.' They want somebody to cook their dinners and darn their socks and no way are the women going to do it. Now, there are some women who probably have to marry or would want to marry for financial reasons. That's no reason to get married. That's a dreadful reason."

Life is problem-solving. What you are about to read are some of the problems to be solved in older-age remarriage and how they were worked out, as told in my interviews with women who remarried after age 50. Being aware of these issues in advance will prevent making an uninformed choice.

Rita is another woman who shared her thoughts with me. Rita has pizazz. Smart and articulate, she knows what she wants and what she doesn't want. She enjoys people, does many things well, and has confidence in herself. I liked her immediately. "Don't assume anything," she said.

Rita is lucky to have supportive family members within a hundred miles of her home. This makes *the* big difference for a single, older person. Having adult children who are a couple of hours' drive away can provide much support to an older person alone.

"I got a divorce from my second husband one year after I married him," Rita told me. "I had been a widow for five years and was in my mid-fifties. I was married to my first husband for thirty-four years, and we had three children. We had a very rich and wonderful marriage. About two years after he died, I began to feel much more whole again, to want to go out with men.

"My second husband talked from the very beginning about marrying me. I fell in love with the idea of living the kind of life I had lived before. It was the idea of being a couple again, of being invited to parties where couples were. I sort of visualized a life much like the life I had had with my first husband, where I had been so happy. So I think that I fell in love with an idea, more than I fell in love with this man. The feeling I had at the time, at this stage in life, was that I wasn't going to wait for two or three years of engagement. I felt I was old enough that if we were going to share any life together, I wasn't going to wait a long time.

"Well, that was wrong. The same thing applies with a second marriage as with a first marriage. You need to get to know that person very well before you make a commitment to marry him. So the fact that I was an older person didn't make it right for me to hurry up the marriage. And I truly think now that had I taken a longer time before setting a wedding date, I might have made a different decision.

"Considering all the baggage that you have with you when you get married a second time — you have children, you have homes, you have a way of life, you have a routine — I think you really ought to have several years of knowing him very well. If you're suddenly thrown together with a man whose personal habits or daily habits are distasteful to you, it can really throw you. If you don't live with him, you may never find out. And you're not as flexible about changing when you're an older person as you are when you're in your twenties.

"I married my second husband fifteen months after I started to see him. We really needed another year or two. He didn't like living alone, so he latched on to me very quickly. His adult children reacted badly at the wedding reception.

"I guess two of the things that I've said are, 'Try not to fall in love with a way of life. Do you really care about him or is it because you think he's going to provide you with something that you're accustomed to?' and, 'Give yourself a long time before you make this big, legal commitment.'"

When an older woman decides to remarry, in addition to adjusting to a new husband who may be retired, she often has to confront the problems created by adult children, even when they live in other states. Usually, the women said, they are the husband's children and their spouses.

There are many ways to confront these issues, both large and small. In my case, I was pleased when my new husband wanted me to teach him how to cook. So I did, and he loves it. He prepares dinner a couple of nights a week. And we enjoy making soup together. These are the things that can help a couple through an adjustment to a new relationship during a phase of life that has many challenges to it.

Six of the women interviewed for the book have success stories, and what these women say offers sound advice and encouragement to those who have found someone whom they want to marry.

I was asked to participate in a National Public Radio program called "Romance the Second-Time Around — After Sixty." The producer, Susan Morris, of Pittsburgh, had interviewed 50 women and men. Based on her interviews, she said the biggest problem is the couple's adult children. I have included a chapter about this important issue facing couples.

Pay special attention to another critical chapter that I have named: "M-o-n-e-y: The Business Side of Second Marriage," which includes information on the one-time $125,000 capital gains tax deduction on the sale of a house, for people 55 and older. This tax deduction may be lost in remarriage. See a lawyer more than a year before marriage — before anyone sells a house.

Don't forget that people need to complete their mourning before thinking about marrying again. For a man, that may be about two years, and for a woman, at least twice as long. Before deciding on marrying again, a wise couple should see a great deal of each other for at least two years, in all situations, not just pleasant dates, and then take another couple of years to work out business and legal affairs. They are *complicated*. You may decide not to remarry after all.

If you think remarriage may not be for you, it doesn't mean the end of a social life! There is a chapter on "Alternatives to Remarriage," with two interesting interviews, that will show you what your options are. You do have choices.

2

REMARRIAGE AFTER 50: IF AND WHEN

IS THERE A BEST AGE?

REMARRIAGES AFTER 50 can work if many steps are taken along the way, before the remarriage takes place. In this book, I try to help people interested in marrying again to sort out the issues that are involved so that they can go into it wisely.

There are questions to ask yourself that each chapter will look at more fully, utilizing the real experiences of the 30 women I interviewed. It is important to appreciate the many concerns that need to be addressed before remarriage, and the elements that need to be in place before you set a wedding date.

You're going to feel vulnerable after a divorce or the death of your spouse. Be sure to allow yourself enough time to heal. Wait at least four years, but preferably longer, before remarrying, just to make sure you're marrying for the right reasons.

If you consider remarrying, what is the best age to do so? I asked the 30 women interviewed, as well as friends of mine who had remarried, this question. All agreed that the best age is in your fifties. The children are out of the nest, sex is still strong and comforting, and you have energy. The husband or both husband and wife are working. There is not the jolt of retirement.

We are more flexible when we are younger — better able to adjust to living with a new person and in a different place.

A widow should know that she will lose her entitlement to her deceased husband's social security if she remarries before she is 60. Hopefully, her new husband will make this up to her.

In sharp contrast, being in one's sixties seems to be the most difficult age to begin a new marriage, because it is the decade of the greatest predictable change. Retirement is near or has taken place. Sex varies for a man, sometimes dramatically, but a woman's desire continues. Health can begin to change. And there is less energy.

It might be wise for a woman over 60 to think about marrying a man one to five years younger than she. This would postpone her problems with his retirement and his potency. One woman I interviewed, **Sarah**, told me she had done that and it had worked out well.

Sarah is alive, with sparkling eyes. She loves to read and play bridge and do volunteer work. She enjoys her friends, both men and women. In addition to her many activities, she keeps in touch with her children. After being a widow for three years, she married a man a few years younger than she, when she was 59. He was divorced.

I liked being with Sarah. She looked me straight in the eye as we talked. I enjoyed her candor. There were still ten years until retirement for her new husband, she told me, which gave her the benefits from his company as well as the opportunity to have "the house and my daytime life to myself."

People marrying in their seventies have accepted the inevitable changes this later phase of life brings and may marry largely for companionship.

Marrying someone in his or her eighties is taking a big chance of caring for a sick spouse. A woman, especially, should have a very good financial arrangement before considering this move, in order to protect herself and her own well-being as she ages.

It's smart to know what you want and don't want for yourself. And it is important to think this through when you are rational, when the healing after a spouse's death or a divorce has taken place, and before you become emotionally involved with someone else. Ask yourself what you want to do with the rest of your life.

Two of the women I interviewed remarried in their mid-seventies and were in their early eighties when I talked with them. Because of their ages, I did not want to call them by their first names, so I have referred to them as "Mrs." with an initial.

Mrs. D. married again when she was 76, after being a widow for five years. Her husband, who was a widower, is the same age as she, and they live in his house. When he was courting her, he gave her a small brown paper bag. She opened it and found the bottom of the bag covered with unset jewels.

A woman with a great deal of energy, she enjoys taking responsibility in her church and other organizations. She likes to drive her friends out in the country and they have lunch together.

Mrs. D. said, "I think the younger you are when you remarry, the easier it is, because the older you get, the more set you are in your lifestyle. And I was pretty set in how I lived. Well, he is, too."

"Marriage is the toughest contract you enter into," said Dr. Heller. "The years after fifty could be wonderful. To make them good, it would be wise to face some of the problems that lie ahead. Have different expectations. Go into it with your eyes open. It will be very different from your first marriage."

3

ADULT CHILDREN:
COMPLICATIONS

THE ADDED STRESSES
THAT PROGENY PRESENT

"EVERY CHILD opposes second marriage for his or her parents," said Dr. Heller. "The structure of the family has changed. One parent is missing. A new person is there. Particularly if there is an estate, children resent having to share it with a stranger to them. They also resent having to share a parent, or feel disloyal to the departed parent."

Dr. Heller touches on many themes in this statement. One of the greatest joys of first marriage is children. They are also the main source of emotional support in illness, old age and death. But in a second or third marriage, one or more of the adult children and their spouses often cause trouble. The stress of this situation can come as a shock to an older, newly married couple.

None of the women I interviewed had adult children from either spouse living at home.

One woman said she and her husband-to-be discussed their furniture. They planned to live in her house. It was decided he would bring half of the furniture from his large house, and she would send half of her furniture to her children. But it didn't work out that way. His children and spouses said they wanted all of it. The woman's children got nothing.

This sense of betrayal can accompany the shock of trying to adjust to adult children who enter the picture along with their widowed or divorced parent. For this reason, it is very important for the couple to confront the issues that may arise at the time they come up, and make an attempt to offset these feelings that will emerge.

As Dr. Heller said, the problems usually come from adult children who did not feel they got enough love when they were young. Those who are secure in their love are happy for their widowed parent who has remarried.

Listen to what Rita, told me. "I had a rather rude awakening one month after the wedding. My new husband's children — adults — came over to my house and created a tremendous scene. And my children came to my defense, but my new husband stood quietly by and said nothing. This was very hard for me. I felt that he should have defended me. I felt that he should have stopped his children from making a scene. They really were berating me, and my own son, the oldest son, wouldn't stand for it, and told them to stop, that they were not to treat his mother that way.

"That incident was a terrible disillusionment to me, to see that the man I married didn't have enough backbone to speak up to his children or to stand up for me. I was really quite miserable. After telling my new husband what I thought about the situation, I stayed up late that night and had a long talk with my son."

These situations are not uncommon, according to experts. For Rita, it had dramatic consequences. "Within a week after that night, I went to see a counselor," she told me. "And I continued to go to see her for several months. But about four months after I married my second husband, I told him I could not stay married to him. In less than a year, we got a divorce."

The adult children may never accept the marriage, even though they may live in distant states. Visits can be ruined by stress and hostility, unless the parent is strong enough to deal with it promptly. One man said, "I can't believe this is my own family," when his adult children and spouses left after a very stressful few days. They had been invited to meet his bride-to-be, who was also visiting him.

Two psychologists whom I interviewed said that in their private and professional lives they had never known of a situation where the sons of a widower 60 years or older have accepted the new wife. Why 60 or more? I asked. Why sons? "Money," they each replied. "By that time, the sons are counting on his money and his possessions."

What is important to remember is that this is a *feeling* on the part of the sons, and feelings — not facts — are what cause problems, psychologists say. If the father has provided for them in his will, or in a prenuptial agreement, there is no cause for this concern that so hinders the relationship with the parent's new spouse. But it still happens. In healthy marriages, money is not a top priority for adult children or their parents.

"Where there are adequate resources, excessive attention to money almost always means a (psychological) problem," said Dr. Heller. "Issues of power, dependency and emotional giving are expressed in monetary disputes."

"Of course, there can be times of crisis in a family where there is job loss, and healthy attention must be paid," he said.

"The second wife is in the worst possible position with her husband's children," said one of the psychologists. She is thought of as a "mother-in-law" and a "wicked stepmother" rolled into one. These negative titles go with the job. It takes a very secure, loving couple to surmount these difficulties together, but many experts say it is usually up to the man to negotiate a good relationship with his children since the problems often arise with *his* children. It is really critical that he openly show his love both for his present wife (or fiancee) and his adult children at the same time. This can reassure them both.

The second wife's children usually are more supportive, probably because they are glad their mother is no longer alone.

Also, she now has someone to help her with decisions and business matters.

Sue, an attractive blonde, smiles easily and is a caring person who gives of herself to other people. She told me she loves square dancing. She is a social worker.

Her first marriage was bad and she got a divorce. Six years later she married again, when she was 55. Her second husband, also divorced for several years, is ten years older than Sue. Expenses have always been carefully planned by Sue and her husband, since money is scarce. They have separate interests, as well as things they enjoy doing together. It is a very good marriage, and Sue and her husband are right for each other.

In Sue's case, she was accepted by her second husband's children, a son and daughter.

"Bill's children are great," she told me. "In fact, I'm very glad that they are here because it gives us grandchildren nearby, whereas my own are far away. I'm very grateful for his family. We like having them over and enjoy their company." Money is not a high priority in this family.

Mrs. D. also experienced a warm reception from her second husband's children and still remembers how, when his son came for their wedding, it was the first time he had met her. "My husband's daughter told me later that when her brother got home, he just couldn't say enough good things about me — he was so pleased."

They *should* be pleased. They no longer have to take care of their father. His new wife is keeping him out of a retirement or nursing home, and he is living in his own house. There's no sex in this relationship. And she's a bargain — less money than full-time help.

If it is possible, it can help to get to know these adult children gradually and to develop a relationship with them that will work.

Janet is a splendid woman. She's the kind of person I would love to have as a close friend. Blond and wearing glasses, she is comfortable with herself. She has a responsible professional position. Divorced, Janet married Jerry, a widower, when she was 53. She had no children of her own, but he had two adult children who lived in another city. After ten years of marriage, this is what she said:

"Jerry has a daughter, and a married son, both in their twenties, who live on their own. His daughter was not happy about our marriage, partly because she had been living with her father until then. I wanted to take his daughter out for lunch, hoping to improve the relationship. He thought I should try. It worked out well. Now we have been having lunch together once a week for a couple of years and the relationship has become a good one. Last summer, the three of us took a two-week car trip together."

From simple lunches to a vacation, a relationship developed. But, it is not always this easy, or possible. Sarah said that "I've gone overboard with his family, to like them all, and do all I can to make it a happy relationship.

"I usually see my family alone. I visit them for holidays and a couple of weeks a year. I enjoy them. He's invited, but he goes to his family. It took us a long time, but we decided it was best for everybody."

This willingness to compromise and come up with a workable solution, even if it wasn't what she hoped for, makes it possible for Sarah, her second husband and all of their children to cope with the stress of a new family structure.

Dot curled up in a large, soft chair in her apartment. She was petite, slender and attractive, wearing shorts. Her short, gray hair had soft curls. She had a relaxed, easygoing manner. I thought she was about 60 and could not believe she was in her late seventies.

"I visited *my* children," Dot said. "He never said I couldn't. (I don't think it would have mattered! I'd have gone anyway.) But he never wanted to have his children visit us.

"When my children came, he was never nasty to me about it, but I knew he was always glad when they went home. I could feel that. I could understand it and I didn't resent it. They'd usually stay a week and that was long enough. My children in California don't feel that way. They think that when I come, I should stay for a month or for three months. And I say, 'I can't stay away from home that long.' But when they come here, it's never that long a visit." In each of these cases, a beloved parent is now being replaced by a virtual stranger.

Sarah and Dot are two women who spend time visiting their children alone each year, without their second husbands. So does **Leah**. As soon as she came in, Leah told me she was a businesswoman. She sat down and proceeded to interview me before she would let me interview her.

"What are you up to?" she asked. When I told her I was a
widow who had remarried when I was older and that I was
interested in the subject of remarriage after the age of 50, she
felt she could trust me and began to talk.

She also was a widow. She and her second husband dated
six weeks and knew they were right for each other — the
chemistry was good. One of their common interests is golf.
He is six years younger than she and was in his fifties when
they were married. They lived together before they were married two years later, and they have a very good marriage.

She said, "Every year I rent a vacation cottage for myself
and my children. During the month my children and I are
together, my husband stays home and plays golf." Each of these
women had previously been widowed and have their own money.
Two of them are completely supported by their second husbands.

I believe an important reason adult children do not accept
the new wife is because they have not completed their mourning
for their own mother. This may take them at least two years,
and it is a necessary process in their healing. The thought of
their father marrying again causes them pain, and they react.
Their father has probably not completed his mourning either,
but does not realize it, and he often is turning to a woman for
the solace he needs. If a spouse had a long illness, some of the
mourning is done then.

But, after a two-year period has passed, the children should
accept courtship. If the man and woman then spend a couple
of years getting to know each other very well before they de-

cide to marry, it will not only help their marriage, but also their relationship with their adult children.

On the morning of my second marriage, my 11-year-old grandson said to me, "This is hard for me, Grandma. I loved Grandpa so much." He had died two years before I remarried. My grandson did not want another change in our family, and he was able to communicate his feelings to me.

All too often, grown children are unable to be so direct. Their feelings are expressed in more subtle ways, and often it is destructive. In addition, their other adult issues — money, sex, feelings of jealousy, struggles with loyalty — come into play.

I never met **Mrs. X.** She left word with the head of a senior citizens' center I had contacted that she would like to have me call her. When I telephoned to make an appointment for an interview, she said, with uneasiness, that she would have to talk to her husband first. Her husband answered the telephone when I called a few days later. I asked to speak to her.

She said her husband would not let her go to an interview because it would cause too much stress. Her words poured out urgently; they were having a bad time. Both were widowed and had been remarried ten years. The stress was caused by his two sons.

They had had a very nice honeymoon, expensive, out of the country. On their return, his adult children said they should not have spent that money. One of his sons has had no contact with his father in the ten years since their wedding. His other son, who lives near them, objects to any extra money they spend and makes their life miserable. She mentioned the word divorce.

They live in her house. She is tired all the time. Now she has health problems.

Her voice was pierced with anxiety when she said, "Tell readers I have heard women say you should not marry a man who has children."

Perhaps her advice is unrealistic, but she is at least issuing a warning that should be heeded. Couples remarrying at this stage in life must beware. In most cases, there will be adult children. As Sarah put it, "I think my life has really differed a lot from my first marriage, and I have to adjust to that. One thing is family, difference in family, and twice as much family, even though they're adults and live in other states. It's twice as much family!"

At least! And sometimes, it is exponentially more than that. It is a lot of adult personalities to mesh, more agendas to figure out and deal with and added stress when two people are trying to simply learn to live together after having lived with others.

4

GETTING ALONG TOGETHER

MARRIAGE IS SO DAILY

C OUPLES CONSIDERING remarriage after age 50 face many challenges. The need for personal space becomes acute in retirement, particularly with a new spouse with whom you have not had time to develop a rhythm of togetherness and separation. The natural flow of awareness of each other's needs takes years to grow. It is a dance of coming together and moving apart.

Kahlil Gibran wrote on "Marriage" in *The Prophet*:

"Stand together yet not too near together:

For the pillars of the temple stand apart,

And the oak tree and the cypress grow not in each other's shadow."

CONTROL ISSUES

Does the other person seem to want to control you? Your activities and interests? Your time? Money? Sex? That is bad news. Run! The person will never change, certainly not at this late date. A controller is a person who is so insecure that he or she has to try to be in control all of the time. Sometimes it can be so subtle that you may not even fully realize it.

Consider what happened to **Carol**. She is an attractive woman of 62 who looks younger. She has smooth, gray hair that she wears in a French twist. She became a widow in her mid-fifties, after a wonderful marriage to an outstanding man. Appearing bewildered that her second marriage is not the same as her first, she wonders if she remarried too soon or should never have married again.

Before they were married, Carol thought she and her husband-to-be had a common interest in art. He had a membership in a famous fine-art museum. But after their marriage, he dropped his membership. So she joined the museum and paid for it from their joint household account. A couple of years later, he canceled her membership without discussing it with her. That is controlling another person. He was controlling many areas of their life, including where they lived. Now she wishes she had recognized other signs of control before they were married. But their courtship was brief. She had let him control that, too.

Each person should be in control of his or her own life. The good mental (that is, emotional) health of each person in a relationship is the most important quality in a marriage.

Janet has had a very different experience from Carol's. She said: "My husband and I feel the subject of control is very important. No one should try to control another person in any way. You should each control your own money, your own time, and what you share and don't share socially. You should have respect for each other's preferences. If he wants to go to a social event to which we have both been invited, and I want to read a book, that is fine with both of us."

The key here is that Janet and her second husband shared this philosophy, and discussed it before they decided to marry. Watch out for controllers! In his book, *Too Perfect* (Ballantine, 1993), Allan Mallinger refers to some men as "neat freaks." Such a man complains about the way his wife keeps the house. Dr. Mallinger believes the obsession for perfection bruises relationships. He says that obsessive people have a powerful, unconscious need to feel in control — of themselves and of others.

A person who is a controller is very hard to live with. Try to look for signs of a situation you would not want to live with for the rest of your life before you marry.

THE NEED FOR SPACE

People need "space" — periods of time alone each day and each week, time to think and grow. But people have different ideas about it. A week alone is wonderful if one likes one's own company, but some people are restless after two solitary days. The issue of space is an important consideration in marriage. Will each partner have his or her own interests and respect the other's need for space?

Space needs differ greatly. One of my sisters and I both need space, but we have different requirements. She spent a week alone in a town in Greece, not even knowing how to speak or read the language. That didn't bother her a bit; she enjoyed it. In fact, she now chooses to live alone. And her personal growth has been enhanced. Another sister had never heard of "space" until we talked about it. Her friends and activities are very important to her.

This is one of the most important differences that can exist between people. One needs to be aware of such differences before marriage. Does the other person like to read books, not just newspapers or magazines? Does the other person like to paint, or listen to music? For many people, a period of quiet time to think and feel is essential.

Dot said: "I think that in second marriages, it is harder for the woman than the man. I think the man can be unaware that we need our space and that we need to assert ourselves. We are used to having the house to ourselves."

There are many ways two people can meet this need. Pat,

who has been widowed twice, said: "My second husband played golf four or five times a week, so I had the house to myself. When we were in Arizona, we played golf three days a week and then he would say, 'What do you want to do? Do you want to go to the race track? Do you want to go to the ball game?' We always did something."

Yet, clearly, Pat felt that she had personal space as well as the companionability of her husband, whom she also describes as a person with a very generous nature.

"If we sat down with a table of eight or twelve people, he would always say, 'What will you have? Waiter, take their order.' And he paid for it. But he himself didn't drink."

There are hints in people's behavior in other situations that can indicate how willing they will or will not be to give you what you need in a relationship. You have to look for them.

One couple I know found a solution to the need for space by each keeping their own homes. Two places to live gives people room to grow. This older remarried couple, who live year-round on a large, popular island, had their own homes about five miles apart. They live together in one, and the other one is for "space" from each other when they need it. They can easily be apart for long or short periods of time. And their children can visit them separately or together. I was amused when they told me about their houses. Now I see the wisdom of their ways.

As for me, I love to wake up in the morning to the sound of my own thinking.

ATTITUDE AND TEMPERAMENT

Is your intended quick to fly off the handle? Are you easygoing, serene? Some people are hard to get along with. You need to evaluate how your personalities mesh. In fact, I recommend reading *Treating Type A Behavior and Your Heart* by Friedman and Ulmer (Alfred A. Knopf, 1984), not for heart problems, but to be aware of personalities. Two Type A's married to each other could lead to in-house fighting!

What happened to Dot was very revealing and is a good lesson in how important it is to look at this aspect of getting along together well enough to get remarried.

"My second husband, Jim, and I went to Hawaii," Dot related.

"He asked me if there was any place I really wanted to go and hadn't been to, and I said, 'Yes, I'd love to go to Hawaii.' He hadn't been there either, although he was well-traveled. He'd had business meetings in different parts of the world and consequently had traveled more than I. We went on a tour to Hawaii with a group of twenty-five or thirty people. All arrangements were made. At the hotel, we ate anytime we wanted and just signed the check.

"A lot of couples in that group went to dinner together, even though they'd only met on the trip. Jim would never eat with them. We were always by ourselves, and I wanted to be with people. When we went on two cruises, it was the same thing. He would never be booked at a table with eight people. He was an introvert. He didn't want people to know about his family. When I'd ask about his mother or father, he'd say, 'Well, what interest is that of yours?'"

Several of the women I interviewed emphasized the need to know a person extremely well and to spend a great deal of time together for at least two years before deciding about marriage. They suggested taking another year or two after that to work out arrangements for a life together.

LouAnne is a good case in point. A petite, attractive Southern woman in her sixties, she was wearing stylish shoes, size four, and carrying a matching handbag. Her daughter, who had introduced us, had said she is always "dressed up."

LouAnne's first marriage had been very good. She was lonely after her husband died, and when she went dancing with her new husband-to-be, she thought life would be good again. She married him eight months after meeting him.

This is what she told me: "I was widowed at sixty-two. I married again five years later, when my new husband was seventy-four. Seventeen months later we were divorced. We had so much fun together while we were dating. But the fun stopped after the marriage.

"We lived in my house. He wanted a larger house, so I bought one. There was no sex. After we got married, his son would not speak to his father. And my new husband did not like my five children or my grandchildren."

Take a good look before you leap, at someone's attitudes and their temperament. The more time you spend together, in everyday living, not just dating, the more you will see. Give the relationship an opportunity to develop. It's better to take longer to make the decision about remarriage.

VALUES

What are your values? Values run deeper than interests, which can change over the years. Values remain the same.

Values are what one cherishes — what one holds in his or her heart. They are the foundation on which one builds. When other things are gone — health, money, even family — one still has one's values. A value is an organizing principle: honesty, trust, kindness, dependability, loyalty, a loving attitude, respect, tolerance of other religions and races, love of family, belief in God, and the power of prayer.

You may place great value on intellectual and cultural things. Perhaps you value music so much that you would "give up your right arm for it," as one musician said. Prisoners of war have said they were sustained by remembering music, poetry, reciting Shakespeare, and prayer.

How you handle money, for example, is not a value. A couple needs to talk about their moral and religious values, which shape their attitudes, before they decide to marry. If one isn't concerned with the needs of others, one can't give to one's partner. A marriage of two people who have the same value system will most likely be harmonious. The next interview confirms this.

The woman I will refer to as **Mrs. K.** was in her early eighties when I met her, and I did not want to call her by her first name. Mrs. K. is a lovely, warm woman. Pleasantly plump, she has eyes that smile and curly white hair. She had been a widow 20 years before remarrying again five years ago. Her husband, older than she, is active and in excellent health. I knew she was happy before she told me. Hers is a love story. I enjoyed her wisdom.

"I think my second husband and I have a very happy marriage," she said. "I was in my mid-seventies and he in his eighties when we were married. I had been a widow for twenty years. I dated men sometimes, but they didn't seem to have the same values that I have, and I didn't look for any lesser marriage than I had before. I was looking for a person who was interested in church, for one thing, and a steward of his money. I was busy during the years I was alone and did lots of volunteer work.

"I had known Paul only slightly when we went on our first date. We found we had the same values."

Valuing commitment helps a second marriage work. In Mrs. K.'s words: "You need to want to make a marriage work. If you see something is wrong in your marriage, you have to say to yourself, 'Well, I can change a little bit.' One person needs to be flexible in a marriage. I don't think you'll get both. My sister also has a very happy marriage. She used to fuss at her husband. Finally she decided, 'He's not going to change.' From that day on, she was a happy woman. She accepted him as he was."

Common Interests

Sharing common interests can be very satisfying, but it isn't absolutely necessary as long as two people accept one another, especially in a later-life partnership when so many interests have been long-standing ones. You may have chosen a person to spend the rest of your life with for other reasons. Dot had a very reasonable attitude about this, I thought.

"I think second marriages should be more fun than first marriages because family responsibilities are behind you," she said. "Since I had such a terrifically good first marriage, I would not put up with anyone who was not good to me. Now I have been widowed twice.

"My second husband, Jim, and I had different interests. I didn't try to make him into my first husband, but I kept missing the companionship my first husband, Henry, and I had. Henry loved to play golf and bridge. I did, too. He was a very gregarious individual. Everyone liked him. Jim was a loner, but he was also a very affectionate man with a good sense of humor, which I enjoyed.

"Jim and I had few interests in common. I missed the companionship of doing things together. If I went out to play bridge or golf, he would always say, 'Go ahead,' but I knew he was waiting for me."

This kind of mutual understanding can really go a long way to make a later remarriage successful. Mrs. D. also found a second husband who was accepting of her activities, even though he did not share her interests. "When I remarried, my new husband said to me, 'I have no intention of interfering with your activities.' He learned that I was very active in church work and that I was president of a volunteer organization. And he has not complained at all when I've been away a great many times during the day."

Pat added that it's not only common interests that keep the love lights burning. "An intellectual match is very important, too. My second husband was brilliant. Of course, I was not a dumbbell either. It was interesting. People would think he was a doctor or lawyer."

When two people also share ideas and thoughts, it can enhance their common ground a great deal. When at least 50 years have gone before, there is fertile intellectual ground to cover!

ENERGY LEVELS

Do you have the energy to create a new, intimate, daily relationship with a different, older husband? And a new social life? It's a package deal. With him or her come another family and their families and friends.

"In older remarriage, a woman takes on the responsibility of showing loving attention to two families in addition to her new husband: his children, including spouses and grandchildren, as well as her own," Sarah told me. "It's twice as much family."

She also cautioned, however, that "the love returned may be missing. Instead, there may be criticism from his family." It takes a lot of mental and physical energy to keep up with this increase in relationships.

Mrs. D. showed a great deal of wisdom in her thoughts about this. "My first husband was ten years older than I. My second husband and I are the same age. By the law of averages, he'll go first, and I'll be high and dry if I've not made preparations — by keeping my friends and looking out for myself financially.

"I've been blessed with almost too much energy. It's important to retain your friendships with your friends, not just his friends, because when he's gone, his friends are going to fade away. When you're first widowed, everybody rallies around and then in a couple of months, boom. You're dropped. So I made it a habit after my first husband died to continue to invite couples for dinner, even though I didn't have a partner."

And then there's the matter of keeping house for two again, at an older age. Juliet B. Schor, author of *The Overworked American: The Unexpected Decline of Leisure* (Basic Books, 1991), says: "Different studies estimate twenty-five to forty-five hours a week doing housework and meal preparation and clean up."

She goes on to say: "Another factor that kept hours long is that husbands desired the services their wives' labor provided. Women were acting, in some sense, as domestic servants. Men liked the fancy cooking and clean homes their wives provided. They encouraged, or even demanded, the service. Men got them free. A housewife is not paid directly for her domestic labor. In a world in which almost every form of labor is bought and sold, why should the housewife's labor be exempted? Had the men been cleaning and cooking, there almost certainly would be less of it.

"Even with men doing more in the home, women are still doing about twice as much housework as men."

Be sure to think about this aspect of a second marriage, and how your own energy level at the stage of life you are in relates to what may be expected of you — or what you expect of someone else.

SEX

Sexual enjoyment, which is a major emotional bond in a good first marriage, is often missing in older remarriage. But giving and receiving loving feelings, touching, hugging and snuggling can go on all of your life.

"Sex" can take many forms of expression. Mrs. K. described it this way: "We have a very happy second marriage and are fond of each other. I never let a day go by without saying, 'I love you, dear.' And that helps. And he says, 'I love you, too,' and kisses me."

Be sure you have the same feelings as your intended about physical and emotional intimacy.

For some people, that would not be a problem. Mrs. D. said to me frankly: "About sex. Well, in our case, you know the old saying, 'If you don't use it, you lose it.' That was a question I asked my second husband before we were married. 'How about sex?' And he said that he could not. 'But if you want it....' I said that I did not. And we have no sex life whatsoever."

There is no right or wrong, normal or abnormal, only what two people are comfortable with and agree to in their most intimate discussions.

Helen Singer Kaplan, M.D., director of the Human Sexuality Program, Payne Whitney Clinic at New York Hospital-Cornell University Medical Center, says that there have been major advances in sex therapy in the last ten years. Many people over 50 are seeking counseling because they realize they are entitled to a good sex life all their lives. She says that most people are sexually active long after they wear hearing aids, and some of her elderly patients are still enjoying good sex — although they can't always remember the name of their partner!

For Leah, in her sixties when she remarried, life with a younger man includes a satisfying sex life. "My first husband died suddenly, when I was in my early sixties," she told me. "I dated my second husband for six weeks, and we knew we were in love. We waited two years before marrying. My children like him and he treats me well. He is six years my junior. We've been married ten years now and have a joyous life together. Sex is fine. It is an important part of our lives."

"If two people are right for each other," she went on, "there is a special feeling, a chemistry between them. I am lucky to have found it in my remarriage."

Sue echoed Leah. "In my remarriage, we do well together. We're right for each other sexually. I think we are a match that way.

Better matched than I was before. And I think we match in the frequency and type of sex that we engage in."

To be in synch with each other, especially as changes occur in later life, is one of the key things couples strive for. Sarah put it this way: "I think it's important to know what your expectations are regarding sex. If you expect a lot of sex and you're married to someone who doesn't, that can cause serious emotional problems. I think you do have to have some compatibility, because sex is with you all the time. It's something you cope with daily, not just once a year. If you don't have a sex pattern or sexual happiness, that could cause a real problem."

She is right. It's this compatibility and sense of keeping it in perspective that will help a second marriage in the sexual area.

Betty, 71, and her husband, 77, have a romantic story.

Betty is easygoing and relaxed. Tall and slender, she has been divorced for 18 years and now is married to the man she had been in love with 50 years earlier. He was widowed for two years when he and Betty saw each other after 50 years. They were married eight months later. Although they had not seen each other in 50 years, they had been in touch every year at Christmas.

"In my remarriage, sex is satisfactory, I guess, some times more than others," Betty said. "But it doesn't play a dominant role."

For Dot, it was a complex area, but she and her husband find other ways to feel physically content. "The frequency of sex in my first marriage diminished somewhat before my first husband died. And I think Jim, my second husband, had indicated before we were married that he couldn't. And occasionally he thought he could, but he couldn't. So it was one of those things. That didn't bother me. There were times when I thought I would have enjoyed it, and other times when I thought it was just as well. Even though we didn't have sex, there was warmth and snuggling and affection."

Pat's description of sex in her marriages reflects the changes couples can experience in a second marriage coming later in life. "Oh, it was a wonderful remarriage," she said. "He loved me so much and he taught me a lot about loving in sex that I never knew. I would never have known, and I think a lot of women go through life and they don't know how nice sex can be.

"My first husband didn't have much of an idea of teaching me about love. I wouldn't have known. My second husband loved women and he wanted to make them as happy as he could, and he did. And I was certainly in love with him and he with me. The first one, too — we were in love, but there were the children and he was climbing the corporate ladder, and it's different."

STRESSES AND HEALTH

"A growing number of researchers are convinced that stress
contributes to diseases, both physical and psychological ones,"
says Dr. Heller in his article on the subject in the Columbia
University College of Physicians and Surgeons, *Home Medical Guide* (1989). He recommends avoiding situations that evoke
hostility. Take your time in arriving at decisions. And try to
anticipate life changes and plan for them.

A stress chart, adapted from T.H. Holmes and R.H. Rahe,[*]
lists 43 stresses in the order of severity. Among the top 11 are:

1. death of a spouse
2. divorce
6. personal illness or injury
7. marriage
10. retirement
11. change in health of a family member

Did you realize that marriage is stressful? When marriage
follows within a year or two after death or divorce, and also
includes retirement, too much stress is piling up. Illness may
well be the result. If you have a choice, try to plan ahead so
you only have one major stress over a two-year period. Marriage can be postponed for a year or more.

---

[*] Adapted from T.H. Holmes and R.H. Rahe, "The Social Readjustment
Scale," *Journal of Psychosomatic Research*, Vol. 11, 1967, pages 213-18,
Pergamon Press, Inc., Oxford, U.K. Reprinted with permission.

ALCOHOL

People have less tolerance for alcohol as they grow older. Many who think they are just social drinkers actually do have a problem with alcohol. With retirement, more leisure, and less energy, it is important to be careful. You cannot drink the same amount of alcohol at 70 as you did at 50.

The latest medical recommendation is to limit alcoholic beverages to one drink a day for women and two for men. There is the same amount of alcohol in 12 ounces of beer, four to five ounces of wine and one-and-a-half ounces of liquor. But there are many people who should not have any alcohol at all. If there is a temptation to have more, it is time to stop completely.

Carol told me, "After we were married, I discovered he had a problem with alcohol. At parties, he always had too much, not at home. I said I would leave him if he did not stop. He stopped completely. But the personality problems remain: compulsive, angry, loner."

OLD AGE

No one wants to think about old age and possible illness. In one's first marriage, your future is your new life together and creating more new lives together.

Perhaps you have already taken care of your first spouse in a long, final illness. It could happen again in your second marriage.

This is what happened to Dot: "When I married Jim, my second husband, he was kind of slow-moving, and it got worse. It finally ended up that he had Parkinson's. Jim kept expecting to feel better and he didn't, and the doctor said that the miracle was that Jim was still alive with all he had wrong with him.

"So the last four years were bad as far as that was concerned. But I didn't resent it. I was glad to take care of him and to do what I could. It was just one of those things. He was up and around. I would still visit my children."

Meeting the challenges of getting along together can make a second marriage an invigorating and satisfying experience. Sue put these challenges in perspective when she told me: "I do think you need to keep negotiation open."

Sue also pointed out that "You can't think of everything ahead of time. You don't know what it's going to be like."

Remember what Rita said: "Don't assume anything."

5

RETIREMENT
AND REMARRIAGE

THE SECOND CHANGE OF LIFE

R ETIREMENT CAN BE DIFFICULT in first marriage,
particularly if the wife is used to having the house to
herself during the day. It is a woman's second change of life.
Older people who remarry have not had the years together to
prepare for it. And they have different children with whom to
spend some of this time if their new husbands have children
from their previous marriage.

Two women who were in their seventies when they married
again said it is retirement that makes the big difference, not age.
Mrs. D.'s husband has nothing to do and is home all the time.

"When a man is retired, a woman loses some of her

independence," Mrs. D. told me. "I think if both people were employed or he was employed and she was not, she would have a greater sense of independence. It's when the man is around. I think it's the man's retirement rather than the age that is hard for a woman.

"I just say to my husband, 'Now, tomorrow, I'm going to the doctor at ten and I'm going to the luncheon at church. There's some turkey soup in the refrigerator for you for your lunch.' I try to have something for him for lunch when I go out so much, and I do go out a lot for lunch. I go out for lunch maybe once a week. I take a couple of older women from church who don't drive. And I'll try to find a new restaurant they've never been to. I take them out to see the fall leaves, and take them out in the spring to see the spring flowers. I never ask him along because he's home taking care of the mail. He sits all day with the mail."

Mrs. K., on the other hand, said: "Life with a retired, older man is different. But my husband is very active, and always out of the house, doing errands and going to the library. Fortunately, his mind is clear. It's very important. He has a good disposition. It wouldn't show before you're married. He does a lot for me. And he goes to the grocery. I think it is retirement, not age, that makes the difference."

She went on to point out: "I think every man likes to be captain of the ship. He likes to make plans. And if it's something I can do, and like to do, I say, 'Absolutely, that'd be wonderful.' We like to take friends out to lunch as our guests. He likes to go out to eat a lot. I just gain weight."

Older men and women remarry for different reasons. An older man may be looking for a "mother" to take care of him, and a "nurse" later on.

Even when the man retires, the woman can never retire, unless some negotiating is done before the wedding bells ring. One woman, who married a retired man, said she is working harder than when she had small children at home. And she is in her seventies. Some retired men try to tell their wives how to run the house!

It is of the greatest importance that a retired man have something he enjoys doing away from the house several days a week. Maybe it will be golf some of the time, but how about a hiking group? Bird watching? Volunteer career counseling in his field of expertise? Volunteer workers are needed in many organizations.

Both people need strong interests and hobbies, like woodworking, painting, golf, tennis, gardening, sailing, reading and bridge. Find out. Is this just talk, or do you see the person taking part in some activities? Travel, which is expensive, does not take up a large proportion of time.

Winston Churchill wrote in *The Gathering Storm*: "To be happy, and really safe, one ought to have at least two or three hobbies, and they must all be real." It's never too late to take up something new, as he did, at age 40, when he began painting. And he loved to build brick walls.

In retirement, there can be less of everything — money, sex, intellectual stimulation from business associates and friends and perhaps each other, and less good health. How you and your possible second spouse will cope with this phase of life is important to explore before marriage.

6

M-O-N-E-Y

THE BUSINESS SIDE OF REMARRIAGE

IT IS ASTONISHING but true that, in the case of a widow:

1. She will lose her entitlement to her deceased
   husband's Social Security benefits if she remarries
   before she is 60 years old. (She can apply for it if
   the second marriage ends.)
2. She will probably lose some or all of her widow's
   benefits from her deceased husband's retirement
   plan upon remarriage. Find out — in writing!
3. She may lose that portion of the estate of her
   husband-to-be, usually one-third or more, which

most states grant a widow, if she signs a prenuptial agreement, according to Francis X. O'Brien, an attorney in Newark, New Jersey. (See "Prenuptial Agreement or Not?" in this chapter.)

For people 55 years old and older, there is a one-time capital gains tax deduction on the sale of the principal residence, not a vacation home. But in remarriage it is very complicated: You may lose it. Timing is very important. A couple is allowed only one deduction. Mr. O'Brien advises consulting a lawyer about the deduction at least a year before remarriage, and before either of you sells a residence; it can work out. (See "Your Place or Mine? Or Another Place?" in this chapter.)

The 30 women I interviewed remarried between ages 50 and 80, and were of middle- and upper-middle-class backgrounds. Their financial arrangements vary greatly in their new marriages. Some women are not protecting their assets. One of the women said, "Think about the financial part. You are losing some benefits. The husband should make them up to you. Find these things out before marrying again. Your financial status is very important."

A marriage is made up of relationships and compromises. The relationship between husband and wife can deteriorate very rapidly if money is a top priority to one of them, or to one or more of their children.

"The love of money is the root of all evil" is from the Bible. This can be even more true in second marriages. There is "his money" and "her money." Probably there are adult children on each side of the family, and these children have spouses. The plot thickens!

In older remarriage, if each partner has three children who are married, that adds up to twelve people, some of whom will be interested in their parents' or in-laws' money. Somewhere in that haystack of adult children and spouses there is likely to be someone who will strike a match. The whole "loving" family relationship may smolder forever, or burst into flames. It takes a very strong, wise couple to be on top of the situation.

Dr. Heller said, "Only the healthiest of children can recognize that their father has emotional needs. Unfortunately, the fear of losing a portion of the estate produces hateful feelings to the 'usurper,' particularly if they haven't gotten enough love from their father."

There are many reasons why people should wait several years before marrying again. Among other things, one needs to be ready to consider wisely, unemotionally, and unhurriedly the depths of a new financial arrangement. It is essential to work out the problems in advance. Money can be the most gnawing subject in older remarriage.

A couple planning to remarry must have a number of serious financial discussions beginning more than a year before the wedding. It's not romantic, but it will help to keep the romance later on. Plans should be made for "our money." The woman should also talk with her lawyer, alone. Her eyes may be opened. Perhaps the man controlled the money in his first marriage and expects to continue now, including telling her what to pay for. Some marriages have been called off at this point.

Money is one of the areas in which a second marriage is different from the first. In the first marriage both partners were young, probably with little money, and they had a common goal. In a remarriage the man may be determined to save money on everything, perhaps to leave it to his children, but this is not always made clear if it is not brought up for discussion. A woman may have some assets, such as her house, that need to be sold or legally protected before the remarriage in order to avoid problems later.

When I married for the second time, I knew nothing about how my remarried friends handled their money. Like sex, it is a private subject. In the interviews I conducted, I was glad to be able to ask the women who had remarried about their new financial arrangements. Mrs. D., for example, told me: "My husband is very generous. He gives me an allowance of over a thousand dollars a month. All I have to do with it is buy food. We live in his house. I sold my house. He pays all the other household expenses — the insurance, the taxes, everything. I have my own car. I bought the car myself, but if I get a big bill, like I'm going to have because I hit a post going into a parking lot and it will cost me almost a thousand dollars to fix it, he says, 'I'll share the cost of that with you.' And when I have a big gasoline bill come in, sometimes he shares that.

"I buy my clothes, and I pay my own doctor bills. And I did that with my first husband, too. Of course, I was working then. But I feel that I am most generously taken care of."

Another couple handles their finances this way: "I put my Social Security check into our joint checking account," Leah said. "We don't buy anything over one hundred dollars without discussion. We own our own house together. We are each executor of the other's estate. I handle the money and write the checks. My money is in trust for my children."

In two other second marriages, both of which are good marriages (of 15 and 30 years, respectively), the couples put their money together, including joint ownership of a new house. Upon the death of one of them, the estate will go to the survivor. When the survivor dies, the money will be equally divided between the couples' children, even when one has more children than the other. All children are to be treated equally.

Janet, who is in her late fifties, said, "I am a professional and make more money than my husband, who is also a professional. But the nature of his work is such that there are occasional times when he is not working. Then I take care of all the expenses, willingly. We did not have a joint checking account at first, but now we do. We keep our other money separately — in our own names."

Sue told me, "I have my money, and he has his money. He pays for certain monthly bills, I pay for certain monthly bills, and we pretty much know what they are. But we are open to negotiate anywhere along the line. If I say I need a new pair of shoes, he'll say, 'Go and buy them. How much are they?' and he'll give me the money to buy them. He knows that I'm very careful. I almost never buy something full price. I wait for a sale. He knows that, and he likes me to look good."

There are many ways to handle finances when you have been in another marital relationship and are forging a new one. Flexibility and good judgment are important. An attorney told me that he has seen cases where the couple in a second marriage put their money together, but there is difficulty after one of the spouses dies. The children of the deceased spouse want their share of the money immediately. They do not want it used to support the surviving spouse, as had been agreed upon in writing in the will. This attorney favors a prenuptial agreement for this and other reasons. He said that the agreement is being used much more today when people remarry than it was 20 years ago.

In another very good remarriage, the husband also provides total financial support for his wife. Since he was working when they were married, his wife will receive his company's benefits for a widow — medical benefits, half of his pension, and his insurance. This is in addition to the benefits she has from her first husband. The second husband wants his wife to save as much of her own money as she can, because she will need it later on. This couple has a prenuptial agreement, but only for the purpose of legally leaving their estates to their own children.

All of the women cited above married men who were still working. Marrying a man who is working is less stressful for the wife. It is easier not to have to adjust to a retired man at home at the beginning of a new marriage. When a man supports his wife in his remarriage completely, she knows he is not marrying her for her money. Some men control the money to their advantage.

Sarah brought this point home when she told me: "I think finances are very important. And the subject of control. My husband feels what's his is his, and I don't get into his finances. And that can be a very sore point. This should be worked out *before* marriage."

Sarah echoed Rita when she said, "Don't assume anything. "I expected that in the house we live in, and I own, he would pay the taxes. But I found out after we were married that he didn't expect to do any of the upkeep or absorb any of the cost of living there. I expected a husband to take care of me in the same way he took care of his first wife."

In general, women live longer than men and will need more money. Older women, over age 65, have almost twice as high a poverty rate (15%) as older men (9%), according to the American Association for Retired Persons' "A Profile of Older Americans" (1993). Perhaps the husband's estate was used up on his last illness. Frequently there is *no* estate. And a spouse usually receives only *half* of the working person's retirement benefits.

The benefits a widow/widower may have from a deceased spouse's company or retirement plan are of great value. Often they continue for the remainder of life. Granted that the figure that was a man's pension is usually reduced to one-half for her, that is still much better than nothing. Medical benefits, which are often without cost to the surviving spouse, are essential.

Does a widow lose these benefits upon remarriage? Many large companies stop one or all of them. Their reasoning: Why should they contribute to support a woman when she now has a husband to take care of her? With the increasingly high cost of medical care, many companies have stopped giving medical benefits to surviving spouses all together. Find out!

The policy can change. Keep up-to-date. A woman thinking about remarrying should review the situation and contact the Director of Employee Relations at her former spouse's employer for complete information. Before remarrying, she should request that the Director put the information in writing. In that way, if she has been given misinformation, she will have legal recourse.

Some couples who are planning to marry find that the widow would lose her benefits, and they decide to live together instead. This arrangement takes understanding on the part of their children and friends.

Listen to Dot's story: "Before I remarried, I told my husband-to-be it was going to cost him money, because before I married him, I still had medical care and hospitalization with the company, and it also paid for medication, and I would lose that coverage when I married him. And also the car insurance, and things like that. He said he didn't care, I was worth it. No, I can't fuss about the money. I told him, 'If you want to marry me, it's going to cost you some money.' I figured if I was going to live on my widow's pension, I was going to live as a widow. I wasn't going to do it any other way. So, anyway, he knew that before we were married.

"For five or six years before we were married, I had a pension from my former husband. And I used it for my travel, for my gifts to the children, and I just kept that for myself. And

I told my new husband, 'I just feel that my income from Henry (my first husband) should be used for my family.' And he never argued, never said anything.

"When we were first married, he paid all the bills and took care of everything. Then he got so that he just couldn't do the physical work of writing, so I took over. The bills were paid with his money. After he died, his daughter got the insurance policy. The rest went to me."

It is very important to find these things out before a remarriage takes place. Pat, who had been eligible for her first husband's Social Security and Navy pension, gave it up when she remarried, and comments that while you need to know these things, it is sometimes hard to find out the information you need. She also stresses that a woman must be aware that sometimes "the man marries the woman and 'eats' *her* money up."

"I have a friend now," she told me, "who married a very prominent man and he had a stroke about three years ago. He was a lecturer and now has no income, and she was a widow. She was a very wealthy woman, but she has him in a nursing home and she said to me, 'It's my money that's keeping him.' He has three children who rarely come to visit him, though they live in the area. She also said, 'Pat, I don't know what's going to happen to me.' She has no brothers or sisters. 'There's nobody in the world to take care of me if I run out of money.' She's scared to death."

There is still an attitude that "A man provides," which affects how many women — and men — view financial arrangements. If both husband and wife agree that this is how it should be, and nothing interferes with it, a comfortable situation can make a second marriage more relaxed, as in Pat's case.

"I was completely supported in my second marriage and any money I had from my first husband I could do with as I wanted," she said. "He told me, 'Spend it on your kids; do anything you want.' And as a result, when they wanted to buy a house, I could give them a down payment. But I did it through my lawyers, with a legal agreement. If there's a divorce and that house is sold, the money has to go back to me. It's all written down."

In addition to the financial issues I have already brought up, there are several more major decisions that must be made.

Your Place or Mine?
Or Another Place?

Starting a new marriage in a different home is good in many ways. It is a new experience for both partners, and they're having it together. Of course, it's a lot of work to move, but there will be fewer old memories. The new couple is getting off to a good start!

Another benefit is that it requires the couple to make a decision on what furniture they want to keep from each home. Their children may be very happy to have what the couple is not using.

"I gave most of my furniture to my children," says Betty. "There's no room for my things. I brought cartons of china, which are in the basement. But the nice part of that was, when I visit my children, it's like walking into my old home. Everything of mine is there — pictures, knickknacks, and such. Many of the things they now have belonged to my grandmother or to my parents."

Carol said, "My second husband sold his house before our marriage and took the capital gains deduction for people fifty-five and older. Because of this, I cannot get the deduction for the duration of the marriage."

She is a good illustration of how, financially, the couple will benefit in a different home if each of them presently owns a home. A certified public accountant I interviewed stated that each spouse will be able to take advantage of the one-time $125,000 capital gains tax deduction for people fifty-five years of age and older, but only if certain rules are followed. Consult your attorney about the deduction *more than a year* before remarriage.

Yvonne underlined the point strongly. Yvonne is an attractive woman 60 years old who looks ten years younger. She dresses smartly, is friendly, smiles a lot, and is easy to talk to. Her first marriage ended in divorce, precipitated by her husband wanting to marry another woman. "He had an eye for women," she confided to me.

She had been alone three years when she met Michael, whose wife had died six months earlier. She met him at a small party in the suburb of Chicago where she lives. Michael lived in Connecticut and was visiting friends. For several days, they spent time together sailing on Lake Michigan, and playing golf. She loved his company. Before he left, he made plans to visit her again.

"Michael, my second husband, sold his house and took the $125,000 capital gains tax deduction," she told me. A year after we met, we were married. We live in my house, so I lost the tax deduction. I wish we had waited a year longer and sold both houses before remarriage. I would have been able to get the tax deduction, and I wouldn't have been surrounded by the memories of my first marriage."

She makes another important point that should start couples thinking about their own feelings apart from the practicality issues. Pat put it this way: "I had a house and I had furniture. I wouldn't have anybody live in my first husband's house, nor would my second husband want to live in that house.

We bought a condo in a suburb of San Francisco.

"I feel that a couple in a new marriage should have a different home. If we had lived in my house, I would be saying *my* house, not *our* house. When you're married, you have to learn to say 'our'."

It is a very individual decision. Betty did not agree with Pat, from her own perspective. "When I went to live in Oregon with Bob, he said to me at the time, 'I will live anywhere.' But I think his home is a lovely spot. He and his first wife were married almost fifty years and had lived there. In fact, they built that house. I wouldn't think of changing it because at this stage of the game, I would much rather have this than my table and chairs and dining room set and things of that sort. In fact, there's no point unpacking my china that is in the basement. I'm very happy with the china that's here."

Mrs. K. told me that she and her second husband do it this way. "We live in his two houses. He has a winter home in the South. I don't contribute to my husband's two houses, which are not retirement homes. That will come later."

As in so many other areas, you have to know your own minds, both of you, examine your pasts and evaluate the pros and cons of the various options. Then work on the solution that is best financially and emotionally.

The certified public accountant I talked to also said that a house is appraised at fair market value at the date of death. When one sells the principal residence, it is mandatory to roll over the gain if one is buying another principal residence. If one is buying a less expensive home, the purchase price of a new home can be combined with the $125,000 exclusion, if it is available to the individual, to absorb some or all of the profit from the original home. She added that it is wise to keep wedding plans flexible to be sure the houses are sold first.

Laws change. They also vary from state to state. See your accountant and lawyer at least a year before remarriage and before either person sells a residence. Be sure to have the most up-to-date information.

Betty is happy with how she and her second husband handled it. She sold her home and moved into her second husband's home. "I cannot sell his house after he dies," she says. "But I have it for as long as I live. And that's fine with me." If just one of the parties sells his/her residence, that person gains an economic advantage that may be resented by the other person. Making a financial settlement at the time gets a couple off to a good start.

PRENUPTIAL AGREEMENT OR NOT?

The decision about whether or not to have a prenuptial agreement is just as important in second marriage, or third, as the decision about marrying! Give this subject top priority a year or more before the wedding. Some marriages have been called off at this point because conflicting attitudes become apparent.

Attorney Francis X. O'Brien said that a prenuptial agreement is not common in first marriage, because usually there is not enough money involved. If one or both parties have some assets in a first marriage, a prenuptial agreement should be considered. A principal reason for having the agreement is that a man and woman can each legally leave the proportion of money each of them wishes to his/her own children. It can also guarantee that a surviving spouse receives a portion of the estate in the second marriage. This should be put into the prenuptial agreement. Unlike separate wills, a prenuptial agreement is **irrevocable**, except by mutual consent. It is a joint legal financial agreement that may or may not outline the minimum **financial** responsibilities of each party.

It is one document, drawn up according to the wishes of the woman and man by the lawyer of each party — usually separate lawyers. If there is to be a prenuptial agreement, it must be signed before marriage.

Work on the agreement should begin a year or so before marriage so that all aspects of it can be thought through carefully and problems brought out and resolved. Perhaps the couple may reach a decision not to have an agreement after all!

The couple should be aware that a widow will not know
her new financial status until her deceased husband's estate
has been settled. This may take three years, even when there
are no complications. There may be very little money if he
had a long hospitalization, particularly if he was too young to
be covered by Medicare. I know a woman who had remarried
before the estate was settled and had signed a prenuptial agreement that she would contribute a large portion financially in
her remarriage, thinking she had ample assets, as her late
husband had indicated. When his estate was finally settled,
she found that most of his investments had been sold to cover
huge medical expenses and taxes. She had been living on his
pension and Social Security, feeling confident that there were
ample assets behind her. There were not.

I conferred with two prominent attorneys, one in San Francisco and the other in the New York City area. They agreed
that the prenuptial agreement is important in older remarriage because:

1. Both parties are required to reveal an inventory of
   their finances at the time of the marriage.
2. It can lay down the ground rules about who takes
   responsibility for what.
3. Each spouse can provide for his/her own children in
   his/her own estate.

The greater the net worth of one partner, or both, the
more important the prenuptial agreement. The wife may or

may not be left money in it by her husband-to-be.

A woman should not rely on a will to protect her financially. A will can be changed every day of the week, and she may
never know of changes, Mr. O'Brien warns. A spouse may
make large gifts to his children. If there is a long illness, there
may be no money left for her after expenses and taxes.

A woman should be aware that if she signs a prenuptial
agreement, she may be giving away her legal right to share
her husband's estate. Most states require that the wife be giv-
en a share of his estate. She should be careful that she is not
waiving her rights in a prenuptial agreement. Most prenuptial agreements cover this topic.

This is how Mrs. D. views it:

"I was brought up to always keep my money in my own
name. So before we were married, we went to his lawyer, and
my lawyer was present. We drew up a prenuptial agreement.
We planned to live in his house. I had to sell my own house,
so that money went into the bank in my name. But I thought,
all right, if he should die first, then I would be left without a
home. So we had it set up that I would have life-right in the
property. That was part of the prenuptial agreement.

"We sought this prenuptial agreement so that I would have
a life-right in the house and so that I would be sole inheritor
of the rest of the property — stocks and bonds — that weren't
in the trust. He has two children. He had a trust for each of
his children before our marriage."

Carol's agreement was similar. "Our prenuptial agreement
leaves money to our own children. I will get income from his

estate for life. The agreement also lists our financial responsibilities. He maintains my house and pays the taxes."

LouAnne had been burned by not having thought of all these angles. Even with a prenuptial agreement, there are unanticipated outcomes sometimes.

"My second husband did not contribute any money," she said. "He would not even pay for food. All he paid for was his own medical care. We had a prenuptial agreement, which said only that he had no right to my money after my death. If the financial responsibilities of each person had been put into the prenuptial agreement, I would have found out that he did not intend to contribute." She got a divorce in 18 months.

Sarah underlined the fact that this is knowledge all parties should have beforehand. "Our prenuptial agreement is only for the purpose of leaving our money to our own families," she commented. "I did not realize we could specify our financial responsibilities for the marriage in the prenuptial agreement."

And in the case of a divorce after a remarriage, the agreement can offer protection.

"I got a divorce a year after the marriage," Rita said. "Because we had a prenuptial agreement, there were not too many complications. We didn't have any community property, and we didn't have any children to support. The divorce became quite simple. It was uncontested. So I would certainly recommend that anybody, even thinking they're going to be married forever, have a prenuptial agreement.

"You may stay with that person forever, but in the meantime, it will protect what you got from your first marriage, so

that your children get it. Before the marriage, when the lawyer showed me the prenuptial agreement, I thought, 'What's
all this stuff in here about divorce?' All I wanted to make sure
of was that my children got what they deserved when I died.
But I blessed my attorney when I suddenly found myself in
the condition of wanting a divorce."

Mr. O'Brien favors having prenuptial agreements drawn up.
He said, "I hope they will put it away [once it is signed]. Don't
let it run your daily life."

Those remarried women interviewed who handle their
money in the same way they did in their first marriages, that
is, either putting it together with their husband's money or
having the husband provide, have truly good marriages and
family relationships, some marriages lasting as long as thirty
years.

Mrs. K. put it this way. "I feel a prenuptial agreement is
very important. We thought about it at the same time and we
decided it would be the thing to do. Our families were pleased.
They never said so, but we could tell by their reactions."
Obviously it is easier on everyone if the agreement makes things
clear to not only the couple, but their adult children also. There
are enough possibilities for misunderstanding, and an agreement can help avoid them.

But not all couples elect to do this. Janet told me that "Jerry and I do not have a prenuptial agreement. He gave some
money to each of his children before he and I married, and
that is all they will get. We are leaving our estates to each
other."

For this couple, the decision was based on other factors and they chose to keep it simple, at least from their point of view.

Another couple also chose this route.

"There was no prenuptial agreement," said Pat, the wife. "He didn't have any family. He had no children. He had two nephews to whom he left tidy sums, but that was it, and they were delighted with what they got. Most of his estate went to me."

While most experts agree that prenuptial agreements are very worth considering, each couple has to decide for themselves.

"Q-Tip" Marital Trust

Couples planning a remarriage should be aware of the "Q-Tip" Marital Trust Law passed in 1982, Mr. O'Brien stated. It is designed primarily for second and third marriages. In this, a man or woman can leave his or her spouse an income for life in a trust. Upon the surviving spouse's death, the unspent principal goes back to the family or estate. This is a marital deduction. There is no estate tax. This is part of the will, and the will can be changed. It is not part of the prenuptial agreement.

COMMUNITY PROPERTY STATES

Nine states have community property laws. Community property is defined slightly differently in each state. These states are not good for couples who plan to keep their money separately. Check with your lawyer if you are going to live in one of these states: Arizona, California, Texas, Idaho, Nevada, Louisiana, New Mexico, Washington, and Wisconsin. Wisconsin was added in 1986.

* * * * *

Nothing I have written is intended to be legal or financial advice. See your lawyer and your certified public accountant for accurate, up-to-date information and advice. And allow lots of time — more than a year. If you can work things out together harmoniously, and you still want to be together the rest of your life, you're off to a good start.

7

ALTERNATIVES TO REMARRIAGE

NOT EVERYONE TIES THE KNOT AGAIN

There appears to be a big risk in marrying again at an older age. Yet divorced or widowed people over 50 are alone. There is a difference between being alone and lonely. Remarriage can have its disadvantages — a widow, for instance, may not want to lose the medical and retirement benefits provided by her late husband's business plan. And she may not want to lose her independence. This chapter suggests alternatives to remarriage.

One alternative is to enjoy a single life and keep the family relationship whole. You will heal, with time, and make a good life for yourself. The holidays will be the same, except for the missing person. You will be able to talk about that person, which you may be criticized for doing with a new spouse present. Pictures of the deceased, which are put away if you remarry, will be on your walls, bringing back happy memories. **Mary** made this choice.

A vivacious woman who was a widow at 62, Mary decided she did not want to marry again because sex would never be the same as it had been with her husband. Her married son and wife and their children live half an hour from her, and she sees the grandchildren almost every week. This is the best support for a single older parent.

Mary said she made up her mind she would have as much fun as she could. She entertains women and married couples, and is asked to join the couples, sometimes travel with them, because she is a happy, positive person.

Another option is living together. This involves all the problems of marriage, plus some disapproval. If the couple does decide to live together, I recommend Johnette Duff and George Truitt's *The Spousal Equivalent Handbook* (Sunny Beach Publications, 1991), which deals with the legal and financial arrangements in such a relationship.

A third alternative is to have a permanent relationship with someone but live separately, which more people are doing. I know two women in permanent relationships, living separately, who have been given diamond rings. When asked about marriage, they say they are engaged to be engaged.

In a permanent relationship you need to have a clear understanding in advance about how serious illness would be handled. Who takes care of the ailing person, physically and financially? This is what works well for **Rachel**.

Rachel, whom I've known very well for 50 years, is a good example of how couples can be creative in making an arrangement that works for them after thinking through what their needs are. Widowed in her mid-seventies, when her husband of 43 years died after a serious illness he suffered for many years, Rachel wrote me a year ago that she had a "friend." This year's letter said, "My friend and I have bought separate condos near each other."

I telephoned her, 3,000 miles away, on weekend rates, and we talked for an hour. She told me all about her life now.

"Two years ago I met Fred, a widower five years older than I.

The chemistry was good, and we took a trip together. Things happened fast. We decided to live together in my house.

"After a few months I found I needed more space to myself. I did not want to be with Fred constantly. And he had a personal habit that bothered me — his table manners. We talked about my need for space and decided to find a place where we could live separately and see each other easily each day.

"We found a beautiful retirement community in the same state, on the water, with lovely gardens. I sold my home of many years (and took the $125,000 house capital gains tax deduction). Fred and I each bought a condo, in separate buildings.

"I love it. He wines and dines and flowers and perfumes me. We have dinner together each night — out. And sex is good. Fred is a gentleman. He adores me and understands my needs. We enjoy each other's companionship.

"The change to living separately was easy for us (unlike divorce) because we had no financial, legal, or medical responsibilities to each other. Medical care is available where we live, at extra cost. The children in both our families think our arrangement is wonderful."

Older-age remarriage can be wonderful, also, when it's the right combination of two emotionally healthy people. I still remember a couple I knew when they were in their seventies, who had been widowed and later remarried. She said, "Today is our nineteenth wedding anniversary, and it seems like we're still on a date."

Epilogue

THOUGHTS TO LEAVE WITH READERS

REMARRIAGE *CAN* WORK OUT

THERE ARE SOME THOUGHTS I would like to leave with you if you are thinking about marrying again.

1. Is each person emotionally healthy? This is *the* most important quality in marriage.
2. Have each of you finished your mourning from death or divorce? Remember: A woman needs several years or more.
3. Are you able to discuss finances intimately?
4. Why does he want to marry you? Remember the

several men in the first chapter who want meals and care? Might he also be interested in your money to live better in his retirement?

5. Does he try to control? How will you have space for yourself? Do you have similar values? (See Chapter 4: Getting Along Together).

6. Remember the alternatives to remarriage in the last chapter.

WAIT (BEFORE REMARRIAGE)

ACCEPT (AFTER REMARRIAGE)

DON'T ASSUME ANYTHING

I remember Leah, the businesswoman, as the woman who did everything right in preparation for her second marriage. They've been married ten years. He's younger than she is, and retired; sex is fine and important to both — there's good chemistry — and he supports her completely. And she spends a month alone with her children each year. She told me, "We have a joyous marriage."

May it be so for you.

BUY COPIES TO GIVE AS GIFTS

Please send me _____ copies of
REMARRIAGE AFTER 50
at $11.95 per copy
$2.00 for postage and handling ($.50 per additional copy)
(Florida residents please add 6% sales tax).

I enclose my check for $ _____

Name _____

Address _____

City _____ State _____ Zip _____

Write for information on discounts with orders of
five or more copies.

Roger-Thomas Press
Box 1563
Fort Walton Beach, FL 32548